Good
Girls
Finish
Last

Good Girls Finish Last

Wicked Words on Drinking, Shopping, Gossiping, Sex, and All Your Favorite Bad Habits

 SARAH PARVIS

A STONESONG PRESS BOOK

Andrews McMeel
Publishing
Kansas City

A Stonesong Press Book

04 05 06 07 08 BID 10 9 8 7 6 5 4 3 2 1

ISBN: 0-7407-4718-5

Library of Congress Control Number: 2004102876

Book design by Holly Camerlinck

Attention: Schools and Businesses

Andrews McMeel books are available at quantity discounts with bulk purchase for educational, business, or sales promotional use. For information, please write to: Special Sales Department, Andrews McMeel Publishing, 4520 Main Street, Kansas City, Missouri 64111.

This one is for the ladies—
all the ladies who stay out until the sun comes up.
You know who you are.

And for my sister, Anne, who knows how to cause trouble
with the best of 'em.

Contents

CONTENTS

To all the ladies who know how to have a good time:

Gone are the days of June Cleaver. Most women are as likely to vacuum in pearls and heels as they are to put on red and blue underwear and a cape and fly around the world saving us from an evil bald guy. (Not that there is anything wrong with colorful lingerie. Or bald men, for that matter.)

There was a time when dainty, demure, and delicate were great compliments, but now, they are just not going to cut it. Strong, sexy, independent, witty, clever, sassy, and fun all beat them by a mile. And the kind of fun I am talking about includes "bad" habits, like bars, men, gossip, chocolate binges, and the phrase "Oops, I did it again."

Dorothy Parker, Mae West, Tallulah Bankhead, and other smart-mouthed treasures have delighted audiences with their praise of vice for years. Here I have collected the witticisms of these saucy women, as well as one-liners from Madonna, Roseanne, Zsa Zsa Gabor, Star Jones, Margaret Cho, the gals from <u>Sex and the City</u>, and other women who know how to sling an epigram and bring a smile to the faces of all female sinners.

These quotes are for the readers who embrace their vices despite warnings by the surgeon general, Dr. Atkins, and their mounting credit-card bills. For us, the hedonistic, happily sinning practitioners of bad habits, Lady Liberty's pedestal might as well read, "Give me your tired, your hungover, your huddled masses yearning to breathe smoke. The guilty overspenders from your 50 percent off sale. Send your drinkers, your chocoholics, your flirts to me. I lift my glass to the party girls, procrastinators, and potty mouths of the world."

So, when you order a pizza and prepare to lounge on the couch with the comfort of your favorite '80s movie, or strap on your trouble shoes for a night on the town, grab yourself a drink, light up a smoke, and take a few minutes with the bad girls on these pages to remember that she who has the most fun wins, and that it's the good girls who finish last.

Cheers,
Sarah Parvis

Justify My Vice

More Fun Than Virtue

"I generally avoid temptation unless I can't resist it."

—Mae West

"Here's a rule I recommend. Never practice two vices at once."

—Tallulah Bankhead

"The trouble with trouble is it starts out as fun."

—Naomi Judd

"Good girls go to heaven. Bad girls go everywhere."

—Helen Gurley Brown

"Woman's virtue is man's greatest invention."

—Cornelia Otis Skinner

"She'd never make the same mistake again;
she always made a new mistake instead."

—Wendy Cope

"Nice girls need to know what a bitch understands."

—Sherry Argov, WHY MEN LOVE BITCHES, 2002

"Fashions in sin change."

—Lillian Hellman

"If I'd observed all the rules,
I'd never have got anywhere."

—Marilyn Monroe

"It's the good girls who keep diaries;
the bad girls never have the time."

—Tallulah Bankhead

"If you obey all the rules you miss all the fun."

—Katharine Hepburn

"The older one grows the more one likes indecency."

—Virginia Woolf

"You don't have to be engaged in questionable or
criminal activities to use an alias."

—Cameron Tuttle, THE BAD GIRL'S GUIDE TO THE OPEN ROAD, 1999

"The feminine faculty of anticipating or inventing what can and will happen is acute, and almost unknown to men. A woman knows all about a crime she may possibly commit."

—Colette

5

"To err is human, but it feels divine."

—Mae West

"Whenever I'm caught between two evils,
I take the one I've never tried."

—Mae West

"If you can't be a good example,
then you'll just have to be a horrible warning."

—Catherine Aird

"You can't deny yourself all pleasures in life. I'm only on about
four or five a day and, besides, I'm going to stop soon."

—Helen Fielding, *BRIDGET JONES'S DIARY*, 1996

"Let's not quibble! I'm the foe of moderation,
the champion of excess."

—Tallulah Bankhead

"Somewhere, and I can't find where, I read about an
Eskimo hunter who asked the local missionary priest,
'If I do not know about God and sin, would I go to hell?'
'No,' said the priest, 'not if you did not know.' 'Then why,'
asked the Eskimo earnestly, 'did you tell me?'"

—Annie Dillard

"Life is a slate where all our sins are written;
from time to time we rub the sponge of repentance over it
so we can begin sinning again."

—George Sand

"Do you want to know what we're good at? There's, um, maintaining when we're fucked up, applying makeup, partying, flirting, making stuff up, throwing parties, having fun . . ."

—*Parker Posey* AS MARY IN *PARTY GIRL*, 1995

"I have bursts of being a lady, but it doesn't last long."

—*Shelley Winters*

"It's queer how it's always one's virtues and not one's vices that precipitate one into disaster."

—*Rebecca West*

"If I had my life to live again, I'd make the same mistakes, only sooner."

—*Tallulah Bankhead*

Smoke This

Cigars, Cigarettes, and the
Love of Tobacco

"Smoking is, as far as I'm concerned,
the entire point of being an adult."

—Fran Lebowitz,
"WHEN SMOKE GETS IN YOUR EYES. . . SHUT THEM," SOCIAL STUDIES, 1977

"I always figured it would be lungs that jumped ship first,
followed a foot behind my liver. It made me happy to picture
myself in an iron lung or an oxygen tent, turning up my
artificial voice box to full blast and screaming at the nurses
to get me a cigarette, goddamnit!"

—Laurie Notaro, THE IDIOT GIRLS' ACTION-ADVENTURE CLUB, 2002

"The only thing I miss about sex is the cigarette afterwards."

—Florence King

"Smoking was about hands the way drinking was about mouths. Unzipping the cellophane and undoing the foil, hitting the bottom of the pack on the side of your hand, shaking out a cig, placing it between your first and second fingers, waiting for a light, holding gently the extended hand that held the lighter, taking the first puffs to make sure the end was lit, inhaling deeply and breathing out slowly to watch the smoke fill the air between you and your companion smoker, tapping the glowing end lightly, watching the ash fall. For some of us, it was better than sex."

—Betty Fussell, MY KITCHEN WARS, 1999

"I sit back down. Light ANOTHER cigarette. GOD. I have to quit smoking one of these days. When I get pregnant."

—Candace Bushnell, 4 BLONDES, 2000

"Hospitals are, when it comes to the restriction of smoking, perhaps the worst offenders of all. Not only because the innocent visitor must invariably walk miles to reach a smoking area, but also because a hospital is the singularly most illogical place in the world to ban smoking. A hospital is, after all, just the sort of unsavory and nerve-racking environment that makes smoking really pay off. Not to mention that in a hospital, the most frequent objection of the nonsmoker (that your smoke endangers his health) is rendered entirely meaningless by the fact that everyone is already sick. Except the visitor—who is not allowed to smoke."

—Fran Lebowitz,
"When Smoke Gets in Your Eyes . . . Shut Them," *Social Studies*, 1977

"Miranda was a huge fan of the Yankees. I was a huge
fan of being anywhere you could smoke and drink
in the afternoon without judgment."

—Sarah Jessica Parker AS CARRIE BRADSHAW IN SEX AND THE CITY

"All I wanted to do was drink my coffee,
smoke my cigarettes, and get the hell out of there."

—Drew Barrymore, LITTLE GIRL LOST, 1990

"But then I do think New Year's resolutions can't technically
be expected to begin on New Year's Day, don't you?
Since because it's an extension of New Year's Eve,
smokers are already on a smoking roll and cannot
be expected to stop abruptly on the stroke of midnight
with so much nicotine in the system."

—Helen Fielding, BRIDGET JONES'S DIARY, 1996

"Now, we've got smokism. It's one of the reasons I became a writer: to be able to smoke in peace."

—Susanna Kaysen, *GIRL, INTERRUPTED*, 1993

"I finally quit smoking by using the patch. I put six of them over my mouth."

—Wendy Liebman

"You wanna see drug-related violence— ban cigarettes in the United States."

—Marsha Doble

"*I* gave up smoking four years, two weeks, and five days ago. But who misses it?"

—Sandra Scoppettone, *EVERYTHING YOU HAVE IS MINE*, 1991

"'Oh, I'm not allowed *chocolate*. Caro and that idiot doctor won't allow it. Or anything else I might enjoy,' she added wryly. 'First smoking, then alcohol, now this. . . . God knows if I give up breathing perhaps I might live forever.'"

—Joanne Harris, CHOCOLAT, 1999

"Sure lighting up a cig is fine for copping an everyday bad attitude. But chewing tobacco—or dipping as it's called in more fashionable circles—is the ultimate bad girl nic hit."

—Cameron Tuttle, THE BAD GIRL'S GUIDE TO THE OPEN ROAD, 1999

"If there could be an alcoholic word for smoking then that would be me. I'm a smokaholic."

—Drew Barrymore

"My roommate Wendi steals my cigarettes. She steals my cigarettes and it creates a rage in me greater and more terrifying than the rage created in me by the thought of an early death caused by many forms of cancer."

—Sherry Kramer, THE WALL OF WATER, 1987

"If you don't keep going forward, you'll roll backwards and crash. And if you stay where you are, you'll never get cigarettes."

—Chyna, ON WHAT SHE LEARNED FROM HER FATHER, IF THEY ONLY KNEW, 2001

"I used to smoke two packs a day and I just hate being a nonsmoker . . . but I will never consider myself a nonsmoker because I always find smokers the most interesting people at the table."

—Michelle Pfeiffer

"The good news: your breath, hair, car,
and clothes won't smell like smoke. The bad news:
if you swallow tobacco juice, you'll puke."

—Cameron Tuttle ON CHEWING TOBACCO,
THE BAD GIRL'S GUIDE TO THE OPEN ROAD, 1999

"And like her hero, Edward R. Murrow, she used her cigarette
to punctuate a question or inhale an answer."

—Betsy Carter, *NOTHING TO FALL BACK ON*, 2002

"I have to smoke more [cigarettes] than most people—
because the ones I smoke are very small and full of holes."

—Beryl Bainbridge, *DAILY TELEGRAPH*, 1996

"People always come up to me and say that my smoking is bothering them. . . . Well, it's killing me!"

—Wendy Liebman

"Apparently there is a Martin Amis character who is so crazily addicted that he starts wanting a cigarette even when he's smoking one. That's me."

—Helen Fielding, *BRIDGET JONES'S DIARY*, 1996

Down the Hatch

Drink, Drank, Drunk

"One more drink and I'd be under the host."

—Dorothy Parker

"I have a giant purse, which we call the movie purse. With it, we can carry in any and all manner of foodstuffs not available at the concessions stand. Like, for instance, margaritas."

—Jill Conner Browne, GOD SAVE THE SWEET POTATO QUEENS, 2001

"What's the point of nonalcoholic beer? This must be for people who *don't* want to get drunk, but *do* want to spend the entire evening in the bathroom peeing their brains out."

—Marsha Doble

SUSAN: A real woman could stop you from drinking.
ARTHUR: It'd have to be a real *big* woman.

—Liza Minnelli AS LINDA MAROLLA
AND DUDLEY MOORE AS ARTHUR BACH IN *ARTHUR*, 1981

"Was really beginning to enjoy the feeling that normal
service was suspended and it was OK to lie in bed as
long as you want, put anything you fancy into your mouth, and
drink alcohol whenever it should chance to pass
your way, even in the mornings."

—Helen Fielding, *BRIDGET JONES'S DIARY*, 1996

"You teach 'em Mother Hubbard went to the cupboard
to get her poor dog a bone. I say Mother Hubbard
had gin in that cupboard."

—Jackie "Moms" Mabley

"There comes a time in every woman's life when the only thing that helps is a glass of champagne."

—*Bette Davis* IN *OLD ACQUAINTANCE*, 1943

"What stops you killing yourself when you're intoxicated out of your mind is the thought that once you're dead you won't be able to drink anymore."

—*Marguerite Duras,* PRACTICALITIES, 1987

"I drank more this morning than an insecure freshman at a little-sister rush."

—*Laurie Notaro,* AUTOBIOGRAPHY OF A FAT BRIDE, 2003

"Even though a number of people have tried, no one has yet to find a way to drink for a living."

—*Jean Kerr,* POOR RICHARD, 1965

"A cup of warm milk sounds kind of good, thanks. . . .
On second thought, just send up a bottle of scotch
and a straw, okay?"

—Cassandra Peterson
AS ELVIRA, MISTRESS OF THE DARK, IN *ELVIRA'S HAUNTED HILLS*, 2001

"Meeting people in bars is simple, mess-free, and it works!
Simply select an establishment and begin ordering drinks until
the love of your life walks in the door. Don't worry if it takes
longer than you expect. Just repeat the pattern until all your
friends and relatives come over to your house one day and
regale you with colorful anecdotes that don't ring a bell."

—Carina Chocano, *DO YOU LOVE ME OR AM I JUST PARANOID?*, 2003

"Liquor is such a nice substitute
for facing adult life."

—Dorothy B. Hughes, *In A Lonely Place*, 1947

"I try not to drink too much because when I'm drunk, I bite."

—Bette Midler

"In a study, scientists report that drinking beer
can be good for the liver. I'm sorry, did I say 'scientists'?
I meant 'Irish people.'"

—Tina Fey, *Saturday Night Live*

"You can't drown your troubles . . . because troubles can swim."

—Margaret Miller, *ASK FOR ME TOMORROW*, 1976

"Sins are the ones you have to give up, not the ones that don't make any difference. Champagne doesn't make any difference."

—Eve Babitz, *EVE'S HOLLYWOOD*, 1974

"CBS chairman Bill Paley came into our dressing room, opened a bottle of champagne, poured the glasses, and said, 'Bottoms up!' I said, 'Isn't that an awkward position for drinking?'"

—Gracie Allen

"Alcohol removes inhibitions—like that scared
little mouse who got drunk and shook his whiskers
and shouted, 'Now bring on that damn cat!'"

—Eleanor Early

"I'll quit coffee. It won't be easy drinking my Bailey's straight, but
I'll get used to it. It'll still be the best part of waking up."

—Megan Mullally, AS KAREN ON WILL AND GRACE

"And never mix your drinks. Stay with one all night long,
like the man you came in with: bourbon, gin, or tequila till dawn,
damn the torpedoes, full speed ahead!"

—Paula Vogel, HOW I LEARNED TO DRIVE, 1998

"Do not allow your children to mix drinks. It is unseemly and they use too much vermouth."

—Fran Lebowitz

"Alcoholism isn't a spectator sport.
Eventually the whole family gets to play."

—Joyce Rebeta-Burditt, *THE CRACKER FACTORY*, 1977

"They're trying to put warning labels on liquor now that say 'Caution: Alcohol can be dangerous to pregnant women.' Did you read that? It think that's ironic—if it wasn't for alcohol, most women wouldn't even be that way."

—Rita Rudner, *WOMEN OF THE NIGHT*, 1987

"Absinthe makes the heart grow fonder."

—Ethel Watts Mumford IN *THE COMPLETE CYNIC*, 1902

"Voluptuous, ripe, and full-bodied, they write.
You can't help but wonder if they've been sampling
wines in bottles, or wenches in brothels."

—Teresa Lust, *PASS THE POLENTA*, 1998

"It is not easy to get an American girl drunk,
and many men have passed out trying."

—Doris Lilly

"A lot of men get very funny about
women drinking: They don't really like it.
Well, I'm sorry lads, but if we didn't get pissed,
most of you would never get a shag."

—Jenny Eclair

"We had moved into a white trash neighborhood specifically so we could spend our leisure time getting drunk and *not* installing sprinkler systems."

—Laurie Notaro, AUTOBIOGRAPHY OF A FAT BRIDE, 2003

"For this and other reasons having to do with women's studies curricula, MTV's programming schedule, and the enduring popularity of alcohol, flirting today falls largely into three categories: defensive, offensive, and drunk."

—Carina Chocano, DO YOU LOVE ME OR AM I JUST PARANOID?, 2003

Excessive Spending

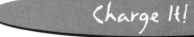

Charge It!

"The price tag on my hat seems to be symbolic
of all human frailty."

—Minnie Pearl

"Anyone with more than 365 pairs of shoes is a pig."

—Barbara Melser Lieberman

"When you are in love with someone, you want to be
near him all the time, except when you are out buying things
and charging them to him."

—Miss Piggy IN HENRY BEARD'S *MISS PIGGY'S GUIDE TO LIFE*, 1981

"I rationalize shop—I buy a dress because
I need change for gum."

—Rita Rudner, WOMEN OF THE NIGHT, 1987

"I have maxed out all my credit cards, their level of
debt now exceeding my annual income, which is not hard to do,
since as a graduate student I make $8,000 a year,
but still, there you are."

—Shannon Olson,
WELCOME TO MY PLANET WHERE ENGLISH IS SOMETIMES SPOKEN, 2000

"Shopping is better than sex. If you're not satisfied after shopping,
you can make an exchange for something you *really* like."

—Adrienne E. Gusoff

"Speak up for the home of the brave. Speak up for the land of the free gift with purchase. Speak up, America!"

—Reese Witherspoon AS ELLE WOODS IN *LEGALLY BLONDE 2: RED, WHITE, AND BLONDE*, 2003

"It was the first female-style revolution: No violence and we all went shopping."

—Gloria Steinem ON THE FALL OF THE BERLIN WALL, *NEWSWEEK*, DECEMBER 18, 1989

"Twenty-seven pairs of kid gloves, in every length and color, were needed to satisfy me before I felt I had enough gloves and indeed, I didn't have to buy another pair for decades. Steve has never gone shopping with me since: the glove episode broke his spirit."

—Judith Krantz, *SEX AND SHOPPING: CONFESSIONS OF A NICE JEWISH GIRL*, 2002

"There is no enticement on earth stronger
than these three words: 50 percent off."

—Jan King, RED-HOT MAMAS: SETTING THE WORLD ON FIRE, 2003

"Nothing speaks of possibilities like a well-stocked
shoe department. Gold hooker spikes, soft-toed ballerina
slippers, Hike-the-Adirondacks boots, run-your-own-firm
suede pumps. It was the Katharine Hepburn *Pat and Mike*,
spectator shoes with their blue tips and white leather
that spoke to me. This was fate at its most obvious;
if I bought those shoes, my life would right itself again."

—Betsy Carter, NOTHING TO FALL BACK ON, 2002

"You can be better dressed when you own a lot of stuff."

—Helen Gurley Brown

"Life's little ills are sometimes best cured by a good dose of shopping. Yet, nary a cure has been found for Compulsive Shopping Disorder (CSD)."

—*THE BAP HANDBOOK,* by Kalyn Johnson, Tracey Lewis, Karla Lightfoot, and Ginger Wilson, 2001

"I'm overdrawn at the bank. I won't say how much, but if you saw it written down, you'd think it was a sex chat-line number."

—Julie Burchill

"Damn straight, I'm a diva, and I've got the attitude to prove it. I've also got the shoes. . . . About three hundred pairs, bought and paid for and occasionally even worn. Out of that three hundred there're maybe thirty that will never see the light of day, but I've got 'em."

—Star Jones, *You Have to Stand for Something, or You'll Fall for Anything,* 1998

"In my imagination, there lurks a man with a glass of red wine whose mission at all times is to spill it over me and ruin the foundation of whatever wardrobe any trip demands. My belief in this possibility means that if I take two pairs of white slacks for a cruise, I need another two pairs as backup to foil the red wine terrorist. . . . My backups, by now, all have backups of their own."

—Judith Krantz, *Sex and Shopping: Confessions of a Nice Jewish Girl,* 2002

"He used to say, 'I read *Playboy* for the articles.' I said, 'Yes, I know. I go to department stores for the escalators.'"

—Rita Rudner, WOMEN OF THE NIGHT, 1987

"If I am wild about a dress, I buy one for now and another to put away so I will still look nice when my career has come to an end."

—Joan Rivers

"I couldn't be out of money. I still have checks."

—Gracie Allen

"I didn't know I could be this happy without incurring credit-card debt!"

—Reese Witherspoon AS ELLE WOODS IN *LEGALLY BLONDE 2: RED, WHITE, AND BLONDE*, 2003

"But it's not the food or the decorating that makes this such a special season. It's the love we all share. Let me share my love and holiday pointers with you at: Neiman Marcus, North Pole; Santa's Rodeo Workshop, Beverly Hills; Wendy's Christmas Living in Wales Shop, Harrod's, where I will be making personal appearances this month."

—Wendy Wasserstein, *SHIKSA GODDESS (OR, HOW I SPENT MY FORTIES)*, 2001

"Every time you open your wardrobe, you look at your clothes and wonder what you are going to wear. What you are really saying is 'Who am I going to be today?'"

—Fay Weldon, *NEW YORKER*, 1995

"It's your intuition that's speaking up when you are drawn to a pink handbag."

—Amanda Ford, *RETAIL THERAPY*, 2002

"I knew I got a bargain for this dress when I heard a lady tell someone that I had gotten it for a ridiculous figure."

—Minnie Pearl

"I'm thinking balls are to men what purses are to women. It's just a little bag, but we'd feel naked in public without it."

—Sarah Jessica Parker AS CARRIE BRADSHAW IN HBO'S SEX AND THE CITY

"OK. DON'T PANIC. Don't *panic*. It's only a VISA bill. It's a piece of paper; a few numbers. I mean, just how scary can a few numbers be?"

—Sophie Kinsella, CONFESSIONS OF A SHOPAHOLIC, 2001

"I always say it doesn't pay to economize. It's the extravagant women who are the most respected by their husbands."

—Fannie Hurst

"I always say that shopping is cheaper than a psychiatrist."

—Tammy Faye Messner

"René always says 'Bonjour, Eloise, voici votre petit déjeuner.'
Nanny always says 'My my my doesn't that look good!'
And I always say 'Bonjour, René, merci and charge it please.'"

—*ELOISE*, BY Kay Thompson, 1955

"I recently went into my closet to grab a pair of black pants and a black top . . . and realized that I have enough black outfits to be the next Johnny Cash!"

—Loretta LaRoche, LIFE IS SHORT—WEAR YOUR PARTY PANTS, 2003

"On my credit cards, I have put dinners and groceries, books, gas, cheap clothes from Target and Marshalls, and expensive boots from Dayton's, which I justified because they were on sale. Mascara, lipstick, nail polish. An eighty-dollar shirt for which I had no justification, except that it is brown, and *brown* is this year's *black*, and all my other shirts are from Target and Marshalls, so I had been *good* and deserved a more expensive shirt, even though I had charged the cheap shirts, too."

—Shannon Olson,
WELCOME TO MY PLANET WHERE ENGLISH IS SOMETIMES SPOKEN, 2000

"You'd be surprised how much it costs to look this cheap."

—Dolly Parton

"One time I love to shop is after a bad relationship.
I go and I buy a new outfit and it makes me feel better.
It just does. In fact, sometimes if I see a really great outfit,
I'll break up with someone on purpose."

—Rita Rudner, WOMEN OF THE NIGHT, 1987

Gold Digger

Go On, Take His Money and Run

"I always said a kiss on the hand might feel very good but a diamond tiara lasts forever."

—Marilyn Monroe AS LORELEI IN *GENTLEMEN PREFER BLONDES*, 1953

"Trust your husband, adore your husband, and get as much as you can in your own name."

—Joan Rivers, REPEATING ADVICE FROM HER MOTHER

"No gold-digging for me . . . I take diamonds! We may be off the gold standard someday."

—Mae West

"I never hated a man enough to give his diamonds back."

—Zsa Zsa Gabor IN THE *OBSERVER* (LONDON), AUGUST 28, 1957

"When you see what some girls marry, you realize how they must hate to work for a living."

—Helen Rowland

"A diamond is the only kind of ice that keeps a girl warm."

—Elizabeth Taylor

"I don't know why women want any
of the things men have when one of the things
women have is men."

—Coco Chanel

"When you are looking for a kindly, well-to-do
older gentleman who is no longer interested in sex,
take out an ad in the *Wall Street Journal*."

—Abigail Van Buren

"Underneath it all, you longed to be annihilated by love, to be
swept off your feet, to be filled up by a giant prick spouting
sperm, soapsuds, silks and satins, and of course, money."

—Erica Jong, *FEAR OF FLYING*, 1973

"I want a man who's kind and understanding.
Is that too much to ask of a millionaire?"

—Zsa Zsa Gabor

"There are a number of mechanical devices which increase sexual arousal, particularly in women. Chief among these is the Mercedes-Benz 380SL."

—Tallulah Bankhead

"She married a man for money and she wasn't real subtle about it either. Instead of her fiancé, she kept calling him her financee."

—Rita Rudner, *WOMEN OF THE NIGHT*, 1987

"Whenever I want a really nice meal, I start dating again."

—Susan Healey

"A gold rush is what happens when a line of chorus girls spot a man with a bank roll."

—Mae West

"I am a marvelous housekeeper.
Every time I leave a man, I keep his house."

—Zsa Zsa Gabor

"I just want a cowboy to ride me home.
I just want a cowboy who's rich and lives in Rome.
I just want a cowboy with gold-plated soap.
I just want a cowboy named John Paul, the Pope."

—Judy Tenuta's LOVE SONG FOR THE POPE,
PERFORMED DURING *WOMEN OF THE NIGHT*, 1987

Oversexed and Liking It

The Sins of the Flesh

"I used to be Snow White . . . but I drifted."

—Mae West

"I'm pure as the driven slush."

—Tallulah Bankhead

"So don't even for an instant consider keeping the following hidden in the back of your closet: a see-through nurse's uniform . . . a cheerleader's costume . . . a little black French maid's outfit. . . . And if you do, don't tell anyone."

—Cynthia Heimel, *Sex Tips for Girls*, 1983

"Personally, I like sex and I don't care what a man thinks of me as long as I get what I want from him—which is usually sex."

—Valerie Perrine

"It doesn't matter what you do in the bedroom as long as you don't do it in the street and frighten the horses."

—Mrs. Patrick Campbell, 1900

"As for the topsy-turvy tangle known as *soixante-neuf*, personally I have always felt it to be madly confusing, like trying to pat your head and rub your stomach at the same time."

—Helen Lawrenson, 1930

"My mother said it was simple to keep a man:
You must be a maid in the living room, a cook in the kitchen,
and a whore in the bedroom. I said I'd hire the other two
and take care of the bedroom bit."

—Jerry Hall

"In my sex fantasy, nobody ever loves me for my mind."

—Nora Ephron

"I will wear whatever and blow whomever I want
as long as I can breathe and kneel."

—Kim Cattrall AS SAMANTHA JONES IN HBO'S SEX AND THE CITY

"I've been in more laps than a napkin."

—Mae West

"A man can sleep around, no questions asked, but if a woman makes nineteen or twenty mistakes, she's a tramp."

—Joan Rivers

"I'm glad I'm a woman because I don't have to worry about getting men pregnant."

—Nell Dunn

"Blow jobs make the world go 'round, just in case
you still thought it was love."

—Jill Conner Browne, THE SWEET POTATO QUEENS' BOOK OF LOVE, 1999

"Safe sex is important. That's why I'm never doing it
on a plywood scaffolding again."

—Jenny Jones

"I've always felt that foreplay should be like a good meal,
going from soup to . . . nuts."

—Cybill Shepherd, CYBILL DISOBEDIENCE, 2000

"By the time you swear you're his,
Shivering and sighing,
And he vows his passion is
Infinite, undying—
Lady, make a note of this:
One of you is lying."

—Dorothy Parker, "Unfortunate Coincidence," Enough Rope, 1927

"I didn't tell him that I would never marry him, because if I had,
the sex would have been over, and I simply wasn't ready
to give up something so good."

—Judith Krantz, Sex and Shopping: Confessions of a Nice Jewish Girl, 2002

"If we always made the smartest choice, we'd never get laid."

—Anna Maxted, *GETTING OVER IT*, 2000

"Men aren't attracted to me by my mind,
they're attracted by what I *don't* mind."

—Gypsy Rose Lee

"When I'm good I'm very good, but when I'm bad I'm better."

—Mae West

"I may not be a great actress but I've become the greatest at screen orgasms. Ten seconds of heavy breathing, roll your head from side to side, simulate a slight asthma attack and die a little."

—Candice Bergen, *DAILY MIRROR*, 1971

"Sex is the Tabasco sauce which an adolescent national palate sprinkles on every course on the menu."

—Mary Day Winn, *ADAM'S RIB*, 1931

"A lady is one who never
shows her underwear unintentionally."

—Lillian Day, KISS AND TELL, 1931

"Sex is good and a good pair of tits is golden."

—Chyna, IF THEY ONLY KNEW, 2001

"It's been so long since I made love
I can't even remember who gets tied up."

—Joan Rivers

"I never married because I'd have to
give up my favorite hobby."

—Mae West

71

"My husband is German; every night I get dressed up like Poland and he invades me."

—Bette Midler

"The way a man chews can tell you loads about the kind of lover he'll turn out to be. Don't laugh—meat is meat."

—Gloria Naylor, *MAMA DAY*, 1988

"If brevity is the soul of wit, your penis must be a riot."

—Donna Gephart

"Those S and M people—they are bossy."

—Margaret Cho, *THE NOTORIOUS C.H.O.*, 2002

"No woman in the world could forget taking control-top panty hose off in the backseat of the car."

—Star Jones, *YOU HAVE TO STAND FOR SOMETHING, OR YOU'LL FALL FOR ANYTHING*, 1998

"Really, that little dealybob is too far away from the hole. It should be built right in."

—Loretta Lynn, ON THE FEMALE BODY

"I'd like to get married because
I like the idea of a man being required by law
to sleep with me every night."

—Carrie Snow

"I'm scared of sex now. You have to be.
You could get something terminal—like a kid."

—Wendy Liebman

"I've tried several varieties of sex. The conventional position
makes me claustrophobic. And the others either give
a stiff neck or lockjaw."

—Tallulah Bankhead

"How do I feel about me?
With my fingers."

—Cher

"Isn't it interesting how the sounds are the same for an
awful nightmare and great sex?"

—Rue McClanahan AS BLANCHE DEVERAUX IN *THE GOLDEN GIRLS*

"When women go wrong, men go right after them."

—Mae West

"She was always pleased to have him come
and never sorry to see him go."

—*Dorothy Parker, BIG BLONDE,* 1929

"What comes first in a relationship is lust—then more lust."

—*Jacqueline Bisset*

"The important thing in acting is to be able to laugh and cry.
If I have to cry, I think of my sex life. If I have to laugh,
I think of my sex life."

—*Glenda Jackson*

"The difference between pornography and erotica is lighting."

—Gloria Leonard

"Girls who put out are tramps. Girls who don't are ladies.
This is, however, a rather archaic usage of the word.
Should one of you boys happen upon a girl who doesn't
put out, do not jump to the conclusion that you have found
a lady. What you have probably found is a lesbian."

—Fran Lebowitz, METROPOLITAN LIFE, 1978

Telling It Like It Is

Attitude, Arrogance,
and Conceit

"But enough about me. Let's talk about you—
what do *you* think of me?"

—Bette Midler AS C. C. BLOOM IN *BEACHES,* 1988

"Sometimes you have to be a bitch to get things done."

—Madonna

"It is the old adjective game, and we reserve the prettiest words
for ourselves. (I'm casual; you're messy; she's a slob.)"

—Peg Bracken

"Don't be humble. You're not that great."

—Golda Meir

"You have no idea how promising the world begins
to look once you have decided to have it all for yourself.
And how much healthier your decisions are
once they become entirely selfish."

—Anita Brookner, *HÔTEL DU LAC*, 1984

"Be arrogant. . . . They won't respect you unless you're rude."

—Martha Graham's ADVICE TO AGNES DE MILLE IN
DE MILLE'S *DANCE TO THE PIPER*, 1952

"The more I see of men, the more I like dogs."
—Mme. de Stael

"Good for the soul—but bad for the heel."
—Agnes Guilfoyle (ON CONFESSION)

"I don't care what is written about me
so long as it isn't true."
—Katharine Hepburn

"Don't fuck with me, fellas.
This ain't my first time at the rodeo."

—Faye Dunaway AS JOAN CRAWFORD IN *MOMMIE DEAREST,* 1981

"Either you've got the goods or you don't,
and if I didn't have the goods I would not have been in
the courtroom, so let's just move on to the next one, okay?"

—Star Jones, *YOU HAVE TO STAND FOR SOMETHING,
OR YOU'LL FALL FOR ANYTHING,* 1998

"Let's face it, if I weren't as talented as I am ambitious,
I'd be a gross monstrosity."

—Madonna

"If you can't be direct, why be?"
—Lily Tomlin

"If your laws don't include me, well then,
they don't apply to me either."
—Mary Stuart Masterson AS ANITA CROWN IN BAD GIRLS, 1994

"Success didn't spoil me; I've always been insufferable."
—Fran Lebowitz

"I am not a saint. I am a noise."

—Joan Baez

"When you was about eight years old, [your mother]
gave you one essential toy. . . . She knew that with this toy,
you would get a swivel in your hips and an attitude to match.
Ladies, when you was about eight years old, your mother
put you outside on the front porch and she
gave you a hula hoop."

—Sommore, QUEENS OF COMEDY, 2001

"Honey, get off the cross. Somebody else needs the wood."

—Dolly Parton AS SHIRLEE KENYON IN STRAIGHT TALK, 1992

"I'll be no man's slave and no man's whore, and if I can't kill them all, by the gods they'll know I've tried."

—Lana Clarkson AS AMETHEA IN *BARBARIAN QUEEN*, 1985

"People honk at me and it makes me have to crash into their car."

—Paula Poundstone

"If you can't say something good about someone, sit right here by me."

—Alice Roosevelt Longworth

**"If you're gonna strut, then strut.
If you're gonna diva, then diva."**

—Star Jones, *You Have to Stand for Something,
or You'll Fall for Anything*, 1998

"I'm an equal-opportunity offender."

—Whoopi Goldberg

"You live but once; you might as well be amusing."

—Coco Chanel

"When this judge let a rapist go because the woman had been wearing a miniskirt and so was 'asking for it' I thought, ladies, what we all should do is this: next time we see an ugly guy on the street, shoot him. After all, he knew he was ugly when he left the house. He was asking for it."

—Ellen Cleghorn

"I punched some bitch in the mouth and her teeth got in the way."

—Courtney Love,
EXPLAINING WHY HER HAND WAS BANDAGED AT A CONCERT IN VANCOUVER

"Did you ever put those maxipads on adhesive side up? Makes you cranky, don't it?"

—Roseanne

"I am 'too fiery'. . . yet I wish to be seen as I am,
and would lose all rather than soften away anything."

—Margaret Fuller

"People will remember that I lived, that I didn't just exist."

—Shirley Temple Black

"A woman's tongue is a deadly weapon and the
most difficult thing in the world to keep in order,
and things slip off it with a facility nothing
short of appalling."

—Elizabeth von Arnim

"When a man gives his opinion he's a man.
When a woman gives her opinion she's a bitch."

—Bette Davis

"12:35 p.m.—The phone rings. I am not amused. This is not my favorite way to wake up. My favorite way to wake up is to have a certain French movie star whisper to me softly at two-thirty in the afternoon that if I want to get to Sweden in time to pick up my Nobel Prize for Literature I had better ring for breakfast. This occurs rather less often than one might wish."

—Fran Lebowitz, METROPOLITAN LIFE, 1978

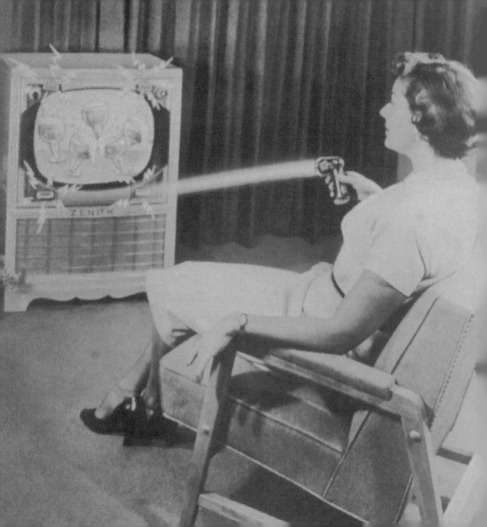

Lazy Daze

The Sin of Sloth

"When action grows unprofitable, gather information; when information grows unprofitable, sleep."

—Ursula K. Le Guin

"Work is the province of cattle."

—Dorothy Parker

"The biggest sin is sitting on your ass."

—Florynce Kennedy

"Walking the mall, I reasoned, was my workout for the day."

—Mo'Nique, SKINNY WOMEN ARE EVIL, 2003

"Jazzercise is fascism."

—Susan Jane Gilman,
KISS MY TIARA: HOW TO RULE THE WORLD AS A SMARTMOUTH GODDESS, 2001

"Exercise is the yuppie version of bulimia."

—Barbara Ehrenreich, "FOOD WORSHIP," 1985

"The only reason I would take up jogging
is so that I can hear heavy breathing again."

—Erma Bombeck

"I have to exercise in the morning
before my brain figures out what I'm doing."

—Marsha Doble

"I'm not into working out. My philosophy: No pain, no pain."

—Carol Leifer

"I have a problem with commitment,
so I decided to become a temp."

—Anita Liberty, *How to Heal the Hurt by Hating*, 1998

"Stand firm in your refusal to remain conscious during algebra.
In real life, I assure you, there is no such thing as algebra."

—Fran Lebowitz, *Social Studies*, 1981

"Now, I want to ask you a question.
How many of you ever started dating someone
because you were too lazy to commit suicide?"

—Judy Tenuta

"I just turned over a new leaf. I decided I'd like to take better control over my life and make sure that less things go wrong every day. So what I've been doing is sleeping up to twenty hours a day."

—Paula Poundstone

"You can't sleep until noon with the proper élan unless you have some legitimate reason for staying up until three (parties don't count)."

—Jean Kerr, PLEASE DON'T EAT THE DAISIES, 1957

"I love sleep because it is both pleasant and safe to use."

—Fran Lebowitz, METROPOLITAN LIFE, 1978

"God did not create this package to work."

—Christina Applegate AS KELLY BUNDY IN *MARRIED . . . WITH CHILDREN*

"Those marathons . . . what would make 17,000 people want to run 26 miles? All I could figure out was maybe that there was a Hari Krishna in the back of them saying, 'Excuse me, can I talk to you? Just a second.'"

—Rita Rudner, *WOMEN OF THE NIGHT*, 1987

"Personally, I have nothing against work, particularly when performed, quietly and unobtrusively, by someone else. I just don't happen to think it's an appropriate subject for an 'ethic.'"

—Barbara Ehrenreich, "GOODBYE TO THE WORK ETHIC," 1988

"My husband says, 'Roseanne, don't you think we ought to talk about our sexual problems?' Like I'm gonna turn off *Wheel of Fortune* for that."

—Roseanne

"Don't let your exercise bikes catapult us back to the days of the buttless monkeys!"

—Lisa Carver, *DANCING QUEEN*, 1996

"Dying's not so bad. At least I won't have to answer the telephone."

—Rita Mae Brown

"I have better things to do—like stay in bed and complain."

—Judy Tenuta

"I'm a writer. A poet. I had the whole day to stay home and write poetry. So what did I do? I got a big cup of coffee, turned on my computer, and played one game of solitaire. Or what I thought would be one game of solitaire. Six hours later and I still hadn't written a thing. But I did win 7 out of 245 games of solitaire. What a day."

—Anita Liberty, *HOW TO HEAL THE HURT BY HATING*, 1998

Housework, Schmousework

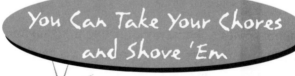

You Can Take Your Chores
and Shove 'Em

"Cleaning your house while your kids are still growing
is like shoveling the walk before it stops snowing."

—Phyllis Diller, *PHYLLIS DILLER'S HOUSEKEEPING HINTS*, 1966

"I hate housework! You make beds, you do the dishes—
and six months later you have to start all over again."

—Joan Rivers

"When it comes to housework the one thing no book
of household management can ever tell you is how to begin.
Or maybe I mean *why*."

—Katharine Whitehorn, *ROUNDABOUT*, 1962

"I am philosophically opposed to ironing."

—Judith Viorst, "TRUE LOVE"

"My idea of dinnerware now is some plastic plates
to eat takeout on."

—Loretta LaRoche, LIFE IS SHORT—WEAR YOUR PARTY PANTS, 2003

"My second favorite household chore is ironing.
My first being hitting my head on the top bunk bed until I faint."

—Erma Bombeck

"Rule of thumb: If it is warm, he'll eat it.
The rest is wasted effort."

—Sherry Argov, *WHY MEN LOVE BITCHES*, 2002

"My idea of superwoman is someone
who scrubs her own floors."

—Bette Midler

"I prefer Hostess fruit pies to pop-up toaster tarts
because they don't require so much cooking."

—Carrie Snow

"I'm not going to vacuum till Se
makes one you can ride on."

"I can't cook. I use a smoke alarm as a timer."

—Carol Siskind

"I figure if my kids are alive at the end of the day,
I've done my job."

—Roseanne

"When men ask me that awful question 'When are you going
to make me dinner?' I say, 'Anytime you like. What kind
of cold cereal interests you?'"

—Rita Rudner, *WOMEN OF THE NIGHT*, 1987

"Untidy is perhaps too mild a word; slut would be a better one. Being a slut is of course partly a matter of bad luck as well as bad management: Things just do boil over oftener, fuses blow sooner, front doors bang leaving us outside in our dressing-gowns; but it goes deeper than bad luck. We are not actually incapable of cleaning our homes, but we are liable to reorganize instead of scrub; we do our cleaning in a series of periodic assaults. A mother-in-law has only to appear over the horizon and we act like the murderer in the Ray Bradbury story who kept on wiping the finger prints off the fruit at the bottom of the bowl. We work in a frenzy; but unfortunately the frenzy usually subsides before we have got everything back into the cupboards again."

—Katharine Whitehorn, *ROUNDABOUT*, 1962

Mirror, Mirror on the Wall

When Vanity Goes Too Far

"Being a woman is worse than being a farmer—
there is so much harvesting and crop spraying to be done:
legs to be waxed, underarms shaved, eyebrows plucked,
feet pumiced, skin exfoliated and moisturized, spots cleansed,
roots dyed, eyelashes tinted, nails filed, cellulite massaged,
stomach muscles exercised. The whole performance
is so highly tuned you only need to neglect it for a few days
for the whole thing to go to seed."

—Helen Fielding, BRIDGET JONES'S DIARY, 1996

"You know, if you want a face peel, you want the
full-strength sulfuric acid skin stripper. It's the total beauty
experience. You know gnarled old oak trees have been
wheeled into this hospital and gone out as saplings."

—Joanna Lumley AS PATSY IN ABSOLUTELY FABULOUS

Mel: Do you know what time it is?
Cher: A watch doesn't really go with this outfit, Daddy.

—Dan Hedaya AS MEL AND Alicia Silverstone AS CHER IN *CLUELESS*, 1995

"Of two evils choose the prettier."

—Carolyn Wells

"All God's children are not beautiful.
Most of God's children are, in fact, barely presentable."

—Fran Lebowitz

"Is it very bright in here or am I badly lit?"

—Kate O'Mara AS PATSY'S SISTER JACKIE IN *ABSOLUTELY FABULOUS*

"Glamour is not for the lazy or the satisfied. It's for the obsessed, the unnaturally ambitious, the ones too bossy to listen when nature tells them what to be. My kind of people."

—Lisa Carver, *DANCING QUEEN*, 1996

"My drawers might be on backwards, but this hair is straight."

—Miss Laura Hayes ON WEARING WIGS, *QUEENS OF COMEDY*, 2001

"Never purchase beauty products in hardware stores."

—Miss Piggy

"My mother's version of natural childbirth was . . . she took off her makeup."

—Rita Rudner

"I'd love to kiss you, but I just washed my hair."

—*Bette Davis* AS MADGE IN *CABIN IN THE COTTON*, 1932

"The rules of hair care are simple and finite.
Any *Cosmo* girl would have known!"

—*Reese Witherspoon* AS ELLE WOODS IN *LEGALLY BLONDE*, 2001

"It's not what I do but how I do it. It's not what I say but how
I say it. And how I look when I am saying and doing it."

—*Mae West*

"Anything you can do to draw attention to your mouth is good."

—Alicia Silverstone AS CHER IN CLUELESS

"My friends ask 'Aren't you afraid of getting killed in the street?' I'm already used to that thought. If it happens, it happens. I just hope if it does happen—I really hope the chalk outline doesn't make me look fat."

—Elayne Boosler, LIVE NUDE GIRLS, 1991

"I refuse to think of them as chin hairs.
I think of them as stray eyebrows."

—Janette Barber

"I loathe narcissism, but I approve of vanity."

—Diana Vreeland

"If I hadn't had them, I would have had some made."

—Dolly Parton

"I'm tired of all this nonsense about beauty being only skin-deep. That's deep enough. What do you want, an adorable pancreas?"

—Jean Kerr, THE SNAKE HAS ALL THE LINES, 1958

"Why you gonna buy titties when you've got socks at home?"

—Adele Givens, QUEENS OF COMEDY, 2001

"Whoever is Jane Seymour's trainer, whoever is the genius who managed to mold her body into a size five Suzie Wong number just seven weeks after she delivered twins, should get the Republican presidential nomination."

—Wendy Wasserstein,
SHIKSA GODDESS (OR, HOW I SPENT MY FORTIES), 2001

"The most common error made in matters of appearance is the belief that one should disdain the superficial and let the true beauty of one's soul shine through. If there are places on your body where this is a possibility, you are not attractive— you're leaking."

—Fran Lebowitz

"I base my fashion taste on whatever doesn't itch."

—Gilda Radner

"Once the people in all countries start having their noses fixed, the economy in those countries will really zoom. Plastic surgery is not cheap."

—Selma Diamond

"The good thing about prison is that you never have
to wonder what to wear."

—Carol Siskind

"Even when I know it isn't true, some little part of me
always clings to the hope that everything would be different
if I just had a new color of lipstick."

—*CATHY* COMIC STRIP BY Cathy Guisewite

"I think onstage nudity is disgusting, shameful, and damaging
to all things American. But, if I were twenty-two with a great
body, it would be artistic, tasteful, patriotic, and a
progressive religious experience."

—Shelley Winters

"I'm getting very comfortable with my body.
I love sleeping on a full-length mirror."

—Sandra Bernhard

"My weakness is wearing too much leopard print."

—Jackie Collins

"I'm not offended by all the dumb-blonde jokes because
I know I'm not dumb . . . and I'm also not blonde."

—Dolly Parton

"I refuse to admit that I am more than fifty-two,
even if that does make my sons illegitimate."

—Nancy Astor

"We have women in the military. But we don't put them on the front lines because they don't know if we can fight. They don't know if we can kill. I think we can. I think all the general needs to do is go over to the women and say 'You see the enemy over there? I just heard them talking. They say you look fat in those uniforms.'"

—Elayne Boosler, *LIVE NUDE GIRLS*, 1991

"The only thing that separates us from the animals is our ability to accessorize."

—Olympia Dukakis AS CLAIREE BELCHER IN *STEEL MAGNOLIAS*, 1989

"Happiness is the sublime moment
when you get out of your corset at night."

—Joyce Grenfell

"When I go to the beauty parlor, I always use the
emergency entrance. Sometimes I just go for an estimate."

—Phyllis Diller

"You look rather rash my dear your colors dont quite
match your face."

—Daisy Ashford, THE YOUNG VISITERS, 1919

Hungry, Hungry Hippo

Love Affairs with Food

"Women should try to increase their size rather than decrease it, because I believe the bigger we are, the more space we'll take up, and the more we'll have to be reckoned with."

—Roseanne

"If your dress size is in the single digits, chances are I'm talking to you. You're evil and need to be destroyed."

—Mo'Nique, SKINNY WOMEN ARE EVIL, 2003

"I was a late bloomer, but once I bloomed, I bloomed big. I didn't understand how the same figure that had served me so well horizontally could serve me so poorly professionally."

—Amy Sohn, RUN CATCH KISS, 1999

126

"I do not overeat because my mother slapped me when I was five.
I overeat because I'm a damned hog."

—Dolly Parton

"I like watching porn and fooling around at the same time.
That's great. That's like eating while watching the Food network."

—Margaret Cho, THE NOTORIOUS C.H.O., 2002

"Great food is like great sex—
the more you have the more you want."

—Gael Greene

"When women are depressed they either eat or go shopping.
Men invade another country."

—Elayne Boosler

"I feel ashamed and repulsive. I can actually feel the
fat splurging out from my body. Never mind. Sometimes you
have to sink to a nadir of toxic fat envelopment in order to
emerge, phoenix-like, from the chemical wasteland as a purged
and beautiful Michelle Pfeiffer figure. Tomorrow new Spartan
health and beauty regime will begin."

—Helen Fielding, BRIDGET JONES'S DIARY, 1996

"Never eat more than you can lift."

—Miss Piggy IN HENRY BEARD'S MISS PIGGY'S GUIDE TO LIFE, 1981

"When did big eaters become the culinary equivalent of sexual deviants?"

—Nina Killham, *How to Cook a Tart*, 2002

"I have gained and lost the same ten pounds so many times over and over again, my cellulite must have déjà vu."

—Lily Tomlin

"Why should we really read the fat and calorie counters on the sides of food packages, either? . . . Once we're fondling a box of Oreos and holding it close enough to read, chances are that we're going to eat them anyway."

—Susan Jane Gilman,
Kiss My Tiara: How to Rule the World as a Smartmouth Goddess, 2001

"The problem with food, of course, is that we can't ever really break up with it."

—Cathy Guisewite, FOOD, 2001

"Everything you see I owe to spaghetti."

—Sophia Loren

"I felt as though everything I ate went instantly to my thighs—like a squirrel storing food in its cheeks."

—Joan Rivers

"The first thing I remember liking that liked me back was food."

—Valerie Harper AS RHODA MORGENSTERN

"I had no intention of giving her my vital statistics.
'Let me put it this way,' I said. 'According to my girth,
I should be a ninety-foot redwood.'"

—Erma Bombeck,
IF LIFE IS A BOWL OF CHERRIES—WHAT AM I DOING IN THE PITS?, 1978

"Once you go fat, you never go back."

—Mo'Nique, *QUEENS OF COMEDY*, 2001

"If you're in any way upset by something—it's a tragedy.
A tragedy demands food, and lots of it. We Queens try to
include items from all four major food groups—
sweet, salty, fried, and au gratin."

—Jill Conner Browne, *THE SWEET POTATO QUEENS' BOOK OF LOVE*, 1999

"What the hell is so attractive about ribs sticking through skin?
Not a damn thing. Now, ribs sticking off the side of a plate,
slathered in barbeque sauce, that's a beautiful sight."

—Mo'Nique, *SKINNY WOMEN ARE EVIL*, 2003

"I am not a glutton. I am an explorer of food."

—Erma Bombeck

"Isn't it time we look at food again for what it is:
sweet sustenance? Of the body and the soul. I say we give
food a break. Stop laying such a trip on it. After all, it's not Jesus,
it's not your therapist, it's not even your mother.
It's just your dinner."

—Nina Killham, *HOW TO COOK A TART*, 2002

"I hate skinny women, especially when they say things like, 'Sometimes I forget to eat.' Now . . . I've forgotten my mother's maiden name . . . I've forgotten my car keys . . . but you've got to be a special kind of stupid to forget to eat."

—Marsha Warfield

"I never worry about diets. The only carrots that interest me are the number you get in a diamond."

—Mae West

"Life is too damn short and food is too damn good to waste time trying to convince folks that I'm worthy of respect simply because the day the good Lord chose to pass out extra helpings of hips and ass, I thought it was a buffet and got in line twice."

—Mo'Nique, SKINNY WOMEN ARE EVIL, 2003

"The preferred way to drink milk is to stand in front of the open fridge and guzzle it straight from the carton."

—Peggy Cullen, *GOT MILK?®: THE COOKIE BOOK*, 2000

"Certainly, in some areas of the world, frying cutlets is a menial task, but in the land of Italian-American-Catholic hierarchy, cutlet frying could easily take the place of beauty and could even forgive a sin as ugly as infertility, especially in a marriage-aged woman with an above-average number of moles."

—Laurie Notaro, *AUTOBIOGRAPHY OF A FAT BRIDE*, 2003

"The acid in diet soda destroys the calories in pizza."

—Valerie Harper's FAVORITE DIET FIBS IN *TODAY, I AM A MA'AM*, 2001

"It's not nice to make fun of fat people—
but, what the hell, they can't catch you."

—Marsha Winfield

"People are so rude to the fat. I go into this dress shop and I ask
this broad, 'You got anything to make me look thinner?' She says,
'Yeah. What about a month in Bangladesh?'"

—Roseanne

"Take away the wigs and the eyelashes and the fabulous clothes,
and you'll find me at White Castle, feasting on a half-dozen of
those greasy square burgers."

—Star Jones, YOU HAVE TO STAND FOR SOMETHING,
OR YOU'LL FALL FOR ANYTHING, 1998

"Spam appeals to some people for reasons other than nostalgia.
Many like it because it contains salt, fat, and sugar—
all the building blocks of good taste."

—Carolyn Wyman, *SPAM: A BIOGRAPHY*, 1999

"Also dieting on New Year's Day isn't a good idea as you can't eat
rationally but really need to be free to consume whatever is
necessary, moment by moment, in order to ease your hangover.
I think it would be much more sensible if resolutions began
generally on January the second."

—Helen Fielding, *BRIDGET JONES'S DIARY*, 1996

"If I had a son of marriageable age, I should say to him 'Beware of young women who love neither wine nor truffles nor cheese nor music.'"

—Colette

"Food is welcome at both meal and snack time. It goes well with most any beverage and by and large makes the best sandwich."

—Fran Lebowitz

"A good cook is like a sorceress who dispenses happiness."

—Elsa Schiaparelli

"You don't have a man, you need spaghetti."

—Oprah Winfrey

"By six years of age I was a fatso who finished her midnight snack just in time for breakfast."

—Joan Rivers

"Terror is the word for facing a day with only eight hundred calories—black ugly terror."

—Helen Gurley Brown

"I'm on the mirror diet. You eat all your food in front of a mirror in the nude. It works pretty good, though some of the fancier restaurants don't go for it."

—Roseanne

Sweet Tooth

For Chocoholics and
Sugar Fiends

"Research tells us fourteen out of any ten individuals likes chocolate."

—Sandra Boynton

"If we love chocolate, is it possible that chocolate helps us to love?"

—Anne Byrn, CHOCOLATE FROM THE CAKE MIX DOCTOR, 2001

"Cookies are the ideal sweet for people on the go. They're hand-held, portable, and easy to eat."

—Peggy Cullen, GOT MILK?®: THE COOKIE BOOK, 2000

"Chocolate is the perfect food because the bliss factor is exactly equal to the guilt factor, and the colliding of the two within the brain uses so much energy that the calories are completely cancelled out."

—Cathy Guisewite, FOOD, 2001

"Nobody diets anymore, it's all exercise. Remember when we dieted in the '80s? The diet that I liked was the Fresca, M&M's, and cocaine diet. That was a great diet, but you can't do that anymore. You can't find Fresca."

—Corey Kanae

"Chocolate: It flatters you for a while, it warms you for an instant; then all of a sudden, it kindles a mortal fever in you."

—Marie, MARQUISE DE SÉVIGNÉ

"Dessert is the crown of the intimate orgy."

—Isabel Allende, *APHRODITE: A MEMOIR OF THE SENSES*, 1995

"Chocolate curls, white buttons with colored vermicelli, *pain d'epices* with gilded edging, marzipan fruits in their nests of ruffled paper, peanut brittle, clusters, cracknells, assorted misshapes in half-kilo boxes. . . . I sell dreams, small comforts, sweet harmless temptations to bring down a multitude of saints crash-crash-crashing among the hazels and nougatines."

—Joanne Harris, *CHOCOLAT*, 1999

"Never accept an invitation from a stranger unless he offers you candy."

—Linda Festa

"I'm kind of a health-food nut myself, thanks. To me, Hostess is one of the four food groups. Though even I don't eat Twinkies. Because they don't have a chocolate outer coating. And so germs can get into the pores of the cake. For me, it is not health food without a chocolate outer coating."

—Paula Poundstone

"The only true rival the Oreo has ever had in the hearts of America is the chocolate-chip cookie."

—Irene Chalmers

"Once you have the taste for sugar, it, like caresses, becomes an addiction."

—Isabel Allende, *APHRODITE: A MEMOIR OF THE SENSES*, 1995

"Ice cream unleashes the uninhibited eight-year-old's sensual greed that lurks within the best of us."

—Gael Greene

"I used to fear that ice cream would be the ruin of me, but I gave up giving it up a long time ago."

—Beatrice Lillie

"I frankly don't understand how people who are genuinely allergic to chocolate manage to put one foot in front of the other, day after day; I'd have to throw myself in front of a bus."

—Jill Conner Browne, THE SWEET POTATO QUEENS' BOOK OF LOVE, 1999

"While other kids were growing up on pizza and Coke, chili dogs and cheeseburgers, I was eating Chocolate. All my life it has been my main ingredient—my passion, my love, and now, my livelihood. All my life I have been on The Chocolate Diet."

—Lora Brody, GROWING UP ON THE CHOCOLATE DIET, 1985

"Energy bars—especially the chocolate-chip coconut—
make you thinner."

—Valerie Harper's FAVORITE DIET FIBS IN *TODAY, I AM A MA'AM*, 2001

"When it comes to drinking milk with cookies,
there are dunkers, sippers, and guzzlers. The type of milk drinker
you are is inspired by the kind of cookie you eat."

—Peggy Cullen, *GOT MILK?®: THE COOKIE BOOK*, 2000

"You want to teach children patience? Leave an
impeccably frosted chocolate cake resting on
the kitchen counter until dinner time."

—Anne Byrn, *CHOCOLATE FROM THE CAKE MIX DOCTOR*, 2001

Potty Mouth

F@*k, S*#t, and Other
Four-Letter Words

"It's hard to be funny when you have to be clean."

—Mae West

"Think with the wise, but talk with the vulgar."

—Greek proverb

"Studies have shown that people who complain live longer.
Yeah, there's always the possibility that this is because the people
who have to listen to them die sooner, but who's to say? . . .
Want health and longevity? Be a pain in the ass."

—Susan Jane Gilman,
KISS MY TIARA: HOW TO RULE THE WORLD AS A SMARTMOUTH GODDESS, 2001

"Wit has truth in it; wisecracking is simply
calisthenics with words."

—Dorothy Parker, WRITERS AT WORK, 1958

"When irritated her vocabulary would . . .
take the feathers off a hoody crow."

—Lillian Beckwith, LIGHTLY POACHED, 1973

"When you say the word B-I-T-C-H out loud,
don't say it like it's a *bad* thing."

—Sherry Argov, WHY MEN LOVE BITCHES, 2002

"There's a name for you ladies,
but it isn't used in high society—outside of a kennel."

—Joan Crawford AS CRYSTAL ALLEN IN *THE WOMEN*, 1939

"I am continually fascinated at the difficulty intelligent people
have in distinguishing what is controversial
from what is merely offensive."

—Nora Ephron, "BARNY COLLIER'S BOOK," *ESQUIRE*, 1976

"Good women always think it is their fault when someone is
being offensive. Bad women never take the blame for anything."

—Anita Brookner, *HÔTEL DU LAC*, 1984

"It's not true that life is one damn thing after another—
it is one damn thing over and over."

—Edna St. Vincent Millay

"Obscenity is too valuable a commodity to chuck around
all over the place; it should be taken out of the safe
on special occasions only."

—Dorothy Parker IN ESQUIRE, 1957

"I rule the land of Wanna-Make-Something-of-It?
where it's always *that time* of the month."

—Anita Liberty, HOW TO HEAL THE HURT BY HATING, 1998

"Swearing is . . . learning to the ignorant, eloquence to the blockhead, vivacity to the stupid, and wit to the coxcomb."

—Mary Collyer, *Felicia to Charlotte*, 1744

"Well-brought-up women didn't say 'fuck' in company in those days, and it seemed to him that I had conviction, energy, and guts . . . and he liked that."

—Judith Krantz, *Sex and Shopping: Confessions of a Nice Jewish Girl*, 2002

"From my lap I'd flip him the permanent bird using a Venus pencil to keep my fingers cocked in place."

—Mary Karr, *Cherry*, 2000

"Ducking for apples—change one letter
and it's the story of my life."

—Dorothy Parker AT A HALLOWEEN PARTY

"Oaths and curses are a proof of a most heroic courage, at least in
appearance, which answers the same end."

—Mary Collyer, FELICIA TO CHARLOTTE, 1744

"Now, on the count of three, everyone say, 'Bitch!'
Feel better now?"

—Courtney Love, LOLLAPALOOZA, 1995

157

"I was just discouraged that one of my fans thought I had a dirty mouth. I said 'But Grandma, that lady said I had a filthy mouth.' She said, 'Come here, baby, let me tell you something. . . . The next time somebody tells you you have a filthy mouth, you let 'em know it ain't what come out your mouth that makes it filthy—it's what you put in there.'"

—Adele Givens, QUEENS OF COMEDY, 2001

"Any woman who can't say a four-letter word sometimes is deceitful."

—Fanny Brice

"I'm a very foul-mouthed young lady. I have a wonderfully dirty sense of humor. I love really dirty things."

—Maya Rudolph

"I have my bitchy side, but don't think I'm really nasty. I think that a lot of other people probably think that I am. Fuck them."

—Debbie Harry

"I have never, ever, been tactless on network television. I save that for HBO."

—Whoopi Goldberg

Don't Worry, I Won't Tell Anyone

The Necessity of Gossip

"Gossip is just news running ahead of itself in a red satin dress."

—Liz Smith

"If I want to find out anything about what's happening in town, on TV, in Hollywood, or in any third-world country, I ask my beautician."

—Jan King, *RED-HOT MAMAS: SETTING THE WORLD ON FIRE*, 2003

"Gossip is the tool of the poet, the shoptalk of the scientist, and the consolation of the housewife, wit, tycoon, and intellectual."

—Phyllis McGinley, "A NEW YEAR AND NO RESOLUTIONS," *WOMAN'S HOME COMPANION*, JANUARY 1957

"Our religions parallel each other. You have confession, we have gossip. What's the difference, really?"

—Elayne Boosler, *LIVE NUDE GIRLS*, 1991

"But it's okay to gossip about other people's sex lives down here in the land of moonlight and magnolia. If you are a Southern woman, it's perfectly okay to brag about your own sex life as long as you use the third person and make damn sure it sounds like someone else's—anyone else's—rather than your own."

—Suzi Parker, *SEX IN THE SOUTH*, 2003

"Men have always detested women's gossip
because they suspect the truth: Their
measurements are being taken and compared."

"The nice thing about egotists is that
they don't talk about other people."

—Lucille S. Harper

"I like knowing more about what goes on than most people . . .
and telling them."

—Katharine Hepburn

AS TESS HARDING TO SPENCER TRACY AS SAM CRAIG IN
WOMAN OF THE YEAR, 1942

"I don't mind men who kiss and tell.
I need all the publicity I can get!"

—Ruth Buzzi

"The idea of strictly minding our own business is moldy rubbish.
Who could be so selfish?"

—Myrtle Barker

"Good gossip is just what's going on. Bad gossip is stuff that is
salacious, mean, and bitchy—the kind most people really enjoy."

—Liz Smith

"Gossip is the opiate of the oppressed."

—Erica Jong

"Show me someone who never gossips and I'll show you someone who isn't interested in people."

—Barbara Walters

"Gossip, like grilling in silly aprons and whining about our cable bill, is as American as it gets. Without it, we'd all wander around talking about the weather or, worse, one another's root canals or inflamed bunions."

—Celia Rivenbark, WE'RE JUST LIKE YOU, ONLY PRETTIER: CONFESSIONS OF A TARNISHED SOUTHERN BELLE, 2004

"It is extremely tacky for a friend to mention a friend's weight to her face. Behind her back is a different thing altogether."

—Cynthia Heimel

"Big-city gossip is just small-town gossip with publicists."

—Carina Chocano, *DO YOU LOVE ME OR AM I JUST PARANOID?*, 2003

"Even the discreetest friends will, like the closest packed hold of a ship, leak occasionally. Salt water and secrets are alike apt to ooze."

—Ouida

"Do send me some gossip. It would be like water to a fish."

—Virginia Woolf

"I hate to spread rumors—but what else can one do with them?"

—Amanda Lear

"I can find out who's cheating on whom, who's dating whom, who's sleeping with whom, and who's in rehab. I ask you— who needs the FBI? In this business, the beauticians have a file on everybody."

—Jan King, RED-HOT MAMAS: SETTING THE WORLD ON FIRE, 2003

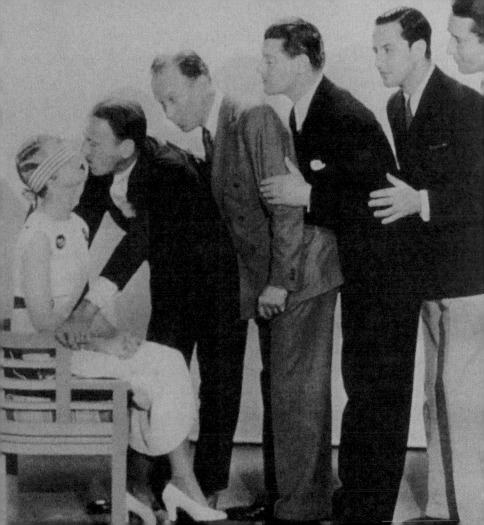

Why Men Are Like Shoes

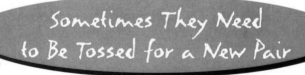

Sometimes They Need
to Be Tossed for a New Pair

"Marrying a man is like buying something you've been admiring for a long time in a shop window. You may love it when you get it home, but it doesn't always go with everything else in the house."

—Jean Kerr, *THE SNAKE HAS ALL THE LIVES*, 1960

"A girl can wait for the right man to come along but in the meantime that doesn't mean she can't have a wonderful time with all the wrong men."

—Cher

"It is possible that blondes also prefer gentlemen."

—Mamie Van Doren

"Being married was like having a hippopotamus sitting on my face."

—Faith Sullivan, *THE CAPE ANN*, 1988

"A Southern Belle's Ten Golden Rules
#5 Never date your sorority sister's ex-husband until at least
three years after the divorce. You might need her to write
your daughter a Kappa Kappa Gamma recommendation one day.
Just remember, it's a lot easier to find a new man
than it is to get your daughter into Kappa."

—Maryln Schwartz, *A SOUTHERN BELLE PRIMER*, 1991

"She always believed in the old adage,
'Leave them while you're looking good.'"

—Anita Loos, *GENTLEMEN PREFER BLONDES*, 1926

"I regard men as a pleasant pastime but no more dependable
than the British weather."

—Anna Raeburn, BRITISH THERAPIST, BBC-TV, 1990

"The only men who are too young are the ones who write love letters in crayon, wear pajamas with feet, or fly for half-fare."
—Phyllis Diller

"Men are those creatures with two legs and eight hands."
—Jayne Mansfield

"Love and marriage go together like angel cake and anthrax."
—Julie Burchill

"I mean, the question actors most often get asked is how they can bear saying the same things over and over again night after night, but God knows the answer to that is, don't we all anyway; might as well get paid for it."
—Elaine Dundy, THE DUD AVOCADO

"The average Hollywood film star's ambition is to be admired by an American, courted by an Italian, married to an Englishman, and have a French boyfriend."

—Katharine Hepburn

"A woman who has known but one man is like a person who has heard only one composer."

—Isadora Duncan

"I can get a husband any time I want. Like *that* woman's husband . . . or *that* woman's husband!"

—Karen Salmansohn,
EVEN GOD IS SINGLE (SO STOP GIVING ME A HARD TIME), 2000

"A man is an accessory like a pair of earrings.
It may finish the outfit, but you don't
really need it to keep you warm."

—Rosemary Mittelmark, 1994

"Living on one's own is not always ideal—
but then, neither is marriage."

—*Barbara Feldon*, LIVING ALONE AND LOVING IT, 2003

"I've married a few people I shouldn't have, but haven't we all?"

—*Mamie Van Doren*

"A woman's appetite is twice that of a man's; her sexual desire,
four times; her intelligence, eight times."

—*Sanskrit proverb*

"The lovely thing about being forty is that you can appreciate twenty-five-year-old men more."

—Colleen McCullough

"I like to wake up each morning feeling a new man."

—Jean Harlow

"Three years into the affair, I was beginning to suspect that couples therapy with his wife must be working."

—Elizabeth Maguire, *THINNER, BLONDER, WHITER*, 2002

"I do have the boyfriend I live with . . . and then the guys I date."

—Ellen Cleghorne, *Def Comedy Jam*, volume 6, 1999

"Women are for friendships. Men are for fucking."

—Kim Cattrall as Samantha in *Sex and the City*

"Get married? Stop having fun? Settle down with just one man?
Life was just starting, for heaven's sake, how could they
not be aching to taste it?"

—Judith Krantz,
Sex and Shopping: Confessions of a Nice Jewish Girl, 2002